Brainwashed to Brilliance
Recovering From Slavery

Mary Ann Wilson

Brainwashed to Brilliance Recovering From Slavery

Copyright © 2021 Mary Ann Wilson

All rights reserved. No part of this book may be reproduced or transmitted in any form or by any means, electronic or mechanical, including photocopying and recording, or by any information storage and retrieval system, without permission in writing from the publisher.

ISBN:979-8-9854584-0-4

DEDICATION

This book is dedicated to my sons, Marion, Manor, my grandsons Makarion and Zyhir. May they all continue stepping into their destiny of brilliancy. May they always know their strength, power and connection to their African heritage.

This book is also dedicated to my beloved and deceased father, Rev. Bennie B. Wilson, who showed me the strength of a powerful Father's influence in my life by taking me to church and helping me understand the significance of being connected to God, my heavenly father.

Legal Disclaimer

This book is Designed to provide information and motivation to my readers. It is sold with the understanding the author is not engaged to render any type of psychological or any other kind of professional advice. The content is the sole expression and opinion of the author. The author shall not be liable for any psychological, emotional, financial, or commercial damages, including but not limited to special, incidental, consequential or other damages. you are responsible for your own choices, actions, and results.

Table of Contents

Introduction 1

Chapter 1: The Psychodynamics of slavery, its impact on our past, present, and future. 5

Chapter 2: A Positive Way of Life and Roadmap to Brilliancy . 23

Chapter 3: Anger management 29

Chapter 4: Positive Self Esteem and Visual Images 41

Chapter 5: The Impact of Spirituality on our brilliancy 49

Chapter 6: The Role of The Black Female 59

Chapter 7: The Role of The Black Male 61

Chapter 8: The Role of the Black Family 63

Chapter 9: Rebuilding the Village 65

Conclusion 69

Section 11 71

Workbook Activity 72

References 93

Introduction

This book addresses the fact that we, as African Americans, have not recovered from slavery. We are still recovering because of systemic racism, white supremacy, health, educational and financial inequality. Many of us are traumatized by what was done to us in the past and is still being done in the present. The mentality of the "Master" may be gone; however, we are still dealing with bigotry, racism, discrimination, and police brutality, just to name a few.

This book gives an abstract overview of where we are as a people in the 21st century. It looks at the history of slavery and how the slave mentality still exists in the mind frame of some people today. As we begin the last quarter of 2021, still dealing with an unprecedented pandemic and the rise in systemic racism, the country is still divided among races. Those who consider themselves superior to other races have begun to increase acts of violence against others. Let's just talk about the big elephant in the room, those who facilitate the mind frame of being superior to any other race in the USA.

People who view themselves as superior to others also have the mind frame of others being inferior to them. These are factual statements; however, the mind frame or belief system is not the truth. When God created man, He never said he wanted one man or woman to be greater than any other. God created man in His own image. Everything God created was good and very good.

The African American race has endured great disadvantages because of the slave mentality. The world view of those who believe they are superior has been to "Keep their knees on our necks" to keep us below their level of education, health, and wealth with well-noted disparities.

The amazing facts indicate opposition to what has been said about the African American population. We have survived the oppression bestowed upon us. Considering the facts, many have been practically blocked out of the American dream of having a piece of the American pie; we are still striving and coming up.

There is a shift in the atmosphere. It's about time for the American pie to be equally sliced among all races. There will be no more of "If you are black, get back, and if you are white, you are all right." We are all God's children, and we all are all right! Many African Americans have been quiet, believing they will be treated fairly. It has not happened for most people of color. It is time for all races to feast at the table, to be treated fairly in this land of milk and honey.

Black females are rising to the occasion and calling to make changes toward equality in America for all races. Black males have suffered tremendously at the hands of white supremacists. Many young Black males who have been oppressed have taken on the role of the oppressor by killing each other. It's time to stop black-on-black crimes. It's time to put down those guns. It is time to spread love and not hate among each other. We are our brother's keeper. We were created to love and not hate each other.

It's time for all young Black males to know their true worth. It is time for all young Black males to step into their true power and recognize their true strength. Knowledge is power. Slaves were brought to

America because they were strong, robust, and hard workers. Many African American males are mistreated because they are so powerful. Some people feel threatened by their strength and power.

There are many reasons for the increase in violence in the African American community. Some may include lack of education, lack of self-pride, social media projections of the black male, history of slavery, police brutality, low self-esteem, poor parenting, absent fathers, drug culture, gang members and lack of motivation to progress from ignorance to brilliancy.

Now is the time to change our thought process to begin seeing ourselves for who we are as a people. We come from a strong heritage of strength, courage, and resiliency. The African American race survived being taken into slavery, separated from families, watching family members being hung, traumatized by slave owners who believed in white supremacy. Slaves were traumatized and exposed to so many other disgraceful things. I cannot mention them all.

We shall continue to overcome the past. We shall recover from our past. Our past wants us to stay sick and maintain a victim's mentality. We are survivors. We are more than conquerors. We are children of the highest God. We are heirs to the throne of God. We are brilliant.

Our job now is to prepare for victory and heal from the hurts of the past. Slavery does not define African Americans. It is a part of our history but not our future.

This earthly life is all about survival of the fittest. African Americans as a race of people have survived. We want to do more than just survive. Many are beginning to thrive. Our job now is to prepare our young boys to become productive self-loving men. I have a regimen to begin our road to recovery. It is a roadmap to stop the violence in future generations in the African American community by brainwashing them into brilliancy.

Let us begin by looking into the psychodynamics of slavery to begin the recovery process.

Brainwashed to Brilliance Recovering From Slavery

Chapter 1
The Psychodynamics of slavery, its impact on our past, present, and future.

Psychodynamic is defined as an approach to psychology that emphasizes the systemic study of psychological forces that underlie human behavior, feelings, emotions, and how they might relate to early childhood experiences. It focuses on the dynamic relationship between conscious motivation and unconscious motivation.

To gain a clearer perspective into slavery, we must not only address how the slaves were treated by owners, but we must also look at how slave owners viewed themselves. Somewhere in the slave owner's childhood, they were taught untruths leading to beliefs about being superior to other human beings. They were not born believing this untruth. It is a learned behavior. The truth is that any learned behavior can be unlearned with conscious motivation.

The conscious motivation behind slavery was to have one race of people believe they were superior to another race. This motivation facilitated the belief in white supremacy and black inferiority.

Personally, as a rational thinking human being, I would not want a race of people described in some history books as lazy and shiftless to work in my cotton fields, pick my cotton, nurture my children, cook my meals, and clean my house. My rational thinking tells me I want someone who is strong, robust, intelligent, hardworking and has the endurance of a strong workhorse working from sunup to sundown.

It is not a coincidence slaves were taken from the continent of Africa. The slave owners knew they were getting people of strength, dignity, and pride. They knew they had to strip slaves of their culture, religion, identity and beat them into submission to become a slave. This was conscious motivation by slave owners.

Slave owners did not know the unconscious motivation of the slaves. Even during the 400 years of bondage, slaves maintained their dignity, ability to survive and rise to unbelievable measures. As is so relevant in the famous poem by Maya Angelou, "Still I Rise."

The past did not define African Americans as inferior. In fact, I can make a conscious statement to say after all slaves endured, they can be labeled as "Survival of the Fittest."

Our past does not define our future. America is still in a crisis and must recover from slavery.

Our present day must confront the pains and residue of slavery, systemic racism head-on to heal a hurting nation. A nation in denial will soon see its demise unless it confronts the pains it caused in the past and continues to cause in the present to African Americans and specifically African American males.

The black-on-black crimes experienced in our communities result from unconscious motivations of slavery. It's nothing new and was birthed during slavery. The slave master used conscious motivation to cause division among slaves. He used the strongest, most robust men slaves to whip, beat and bring other slaves into submission to the slave master's rules and guidelines. The slave masters used skin tones as conscious motivation to cause divisions among slaves. Slave masters used what they termed as "field and house niggas" to cause division among slaves.

Today in America, we live in retrospect in our high crime areas in the black community. Black men are killing each other at extremely high rates. This act can be considered a result of the slave masters' actions of unconscious motivation for future generations of African American males. The black-on-black crimes in our neighborhoods can be viewed as the continued evolution of slavery and slave mentality.

Let us begin to look at the paradigm of how African American males in the ghetto begin to heal from slavery. Let us teach them ways to realize their true powers of brilliancy. They are born brilliant, and no one has told the ones who are killing each other they can overcome the slave mentality and live a productive crime-free life. They believe the negative images they see of themselves portrayed on television, social media, and newspapers. They have a poor self-image and low self-esteem. They are likely to be uneducated as well.

So now we know where the problem started. Let's look at solutions and ways to consciously motivate and effect positive changes within our communities. Let's get brainwashed to Brilliancy.

Even though many people still have the slave mentality because some of the same symptomologies of slavery still exist today. We can begin to heal by implementing a recovery plan.

Recovery is an ongoing process continuing throughout the life process. Let us start healing from the past and begin anew. Let us begin stepping into our brilliancy by following the steps of a recovery plan listed below.

1. **First, we must Love ourselves as God loves us.**

It is difficult to love oneself while hearing negative talk or seeing negative imagines of yourself daily. Our self-image and beliefs about ourselves are learned during childhood. When a child hears positive talk and receives positive rewards, he will begin to feel good about himself. He will believe he can do positive things. He will grow into his brilliancy.

Growing up, I believed we were poor because my parents married as teenagers, had five children, and divorced after being married for five years. We lived in a two-bedroom house where all the children slept in the same bed. My daddy worked and brought groceries home. My daddy worked for white folks. As a child, I believed only white folks were rich.

My daddy would tell us stories about how his boss man would leave dimes and nickels on a table to see if he would pick up the money. My daddy said he would never pick up the money. He stated he would add a dime or nickel to the money to prove to his boss he didn't steal. Looking back on this example now, I think it was a brilliant idea.

After my parents divorced, my mom, four siblings, and I lived with my grandparents for a while. My mom eventually moved to New York with relatives leaving my siblings and me, except the baby girl, living with my grandparents. She took the baby with her. My four siblings and I slept on a pallet on the floor in my grandparents' living room until my mother returned and remarried.

I was sexually molested by a male relative at age five while living with my grandparents, developed a poor self-imagine, and felt a sense of worthlessness because I felt I was not safe and protected from abuse by those who were supposed to protect my siblings and me.

I developed a lack of trust in the men who were supposed to

protect me but had left me open to undue pain and suffering.

I developed a poor self-image during my pre-teen years. The abuse left a devastating impact on me.

I compared myself to the pretty white girls with long flowing hair. I felt I didn't measure up to what I was brainwashed to believe how beauty was defined by what was portrayed in magazines and television ads. I felt inferior and unattractive because of being black and poor.

Once I started middle school, I began to feel more positive about myself. My self-image began to improve. My friends started calling me cute. I was selected by my peers as a class beauty and class favorite.

I was very critical of my looks. I remember thinking my nose was too big on my face. I later learned to accept my physical features as a gift from God because I was created in His image. I also realized my biological family may have been poor financially, but we were rich in integrity and dignity despite the struggles we endured.

My self-love increased when I matriculated at Tuskegee University. I was around people who made me feel "Black and Proud" every day.

Contrary to what I learned in high school, I embraced my rich heritage feeling proud of my history instead of ashamed of it. I loved myself more because of my struggles. My worldview changed. I viewed myself as a strong person instead of a weak person because of the history of slavery impacting African American lives. I became a little more militant in my beliefs about my race. I began to love myself, embracing all my history, regardless of the pains and suffering African Americans endured in the past and continue to endure in the 21st century.

My professors and instructors at Tuskegee University were nurturing, motivating me to be very proud of my blackness and heritage. I learned more about my culture. I was exposed to people from all over the world. I was also introduced to students from international backgrounds. I met students and instructors from foreign countries. I met my first person from Africa.

Contrary to what was portrayed on television about people from Africa, I was intrigued by meeting students from Africa who were some of the most intelligent students on campus. American social media brainwashed some African Americans into believing Africans were uncivilized people swinging from trees like the scenes in the movie Tarzan.

I often wondered about Africa and what it would have been like being raised in Africa instead of having the legacy of slavery following African Americans like a noose around our necks every day of our lives.

My worldview about my heritage changed from negative to positive during my matriculation at Tuskegee University. I began to understand African Americans are brilliant and intelligent instead of what had been portrayed about us in the news and newspapers.

My self-image began to soar. I was being brainwashed from ignorance to brilliancy. I also learned ignorant is not a bad word. It simply means lacking knowledge or awareness in general; uneducated or unsophisticated.

2. **Teach children education is one of the keys to a successful life:**

Knowledge is power. Brilliancy begins when we begin to learn our true powers. Each of us has our own magical powers. We are fearfully and wonderfully made according to Psalm 139:14.

During my formative years, I attended Van Buren Elementary School before the schools were desegregated in 1968 after Dr. Martin Luther King was killed. During my elementary school years, my teachers brainwashed the students with the idea that a college education was the key to having a successful life. They made sure students learned what they needed to be smart and successful. They were very strict and disciplined about student learning.

Those were the days when students respected teachers and teachers respected the children holding them accountable for their actions and behaviors. Parents were very strict about children learning and getting a good education. Teachers were well respected in the community. Parents would listen to teachers and discipline their children accordingly.

People who are educated have a sense of dignity and accomplishment. As I became a college graduate, I learned that education affords the opportunity to compete in a competitive job market. Most college graduates are far better financially than those without a college degree, with few exceptions.

As a young child, I always heard the phrase, "Education is the key to a successful future. You need to get a good education to be successful and get out of the ghetto." I was brainwashed to believe getting a good education was the key to having a successful life.

My parents did not receive a high school education but were adamant about their children going to school and completing high school. They ensured my siblings and I had adequate school supplies, new school clothing and shoes each year.

As I recall my first day of school, I remember being so afraid and not wanting my older sister to leave me after we walked into the schoolhouse at Van Buren Elementary School. I remember pulling on her hand while crying when she was leaving me to go to her second-grade class. I was supposed to be going to my first-grade class. Eventually, one of the teachers took me by the hand, pulled me away from my sister and took me to my first-grade class. I was afraid of school initially.

I became adjusted to school after a while. I thought all the schoolteachers were very pretty. They dressed professionally and walked with authority and dignity.

They were nice and kind. They were adamant about students learning what was expected. I did well in my elementary school years. I attended an all-Black school my first five years.

I was excited to be going to an all-black middle-high school called TV McCoo High School for grades 6 through 12th. I would hear my older sister talk about the high school games and how the band performed at the games. I would get a glimpse of the excitement of the band's performance during the homecoming parades at downtown Eufaula. It was a big event when there was a parade downtown.

Attending an all-Black elementary school prepared me for the new world I was about to embrace. The world was changing after Dr. Martin Luther King was assassinated on April 4, 1968. I completed my fifth-grade year at an all-Black school where we were brainwashed into believing a good education was the key to success. We were brainwashed into brilliancy.

At age 11, I attended Admiral Moore Middle School in my hometown of Eufaula. Many of the schools in Alabama were desegregated, with black and white children attending public school together by this time. It was designed to give Blacks a better education and more equal opportunities. I was able to acclimate to the new school even though I felt disappointed I would not experience attending the football games to see the band's performance during the halftime show at TV McCoo High School.

It was quite a change attending the new school. Most of the teachers were white except for a few Black teachers I knew from attending my all-Black elementary school. This was the year when the movie "Roots" came out. There were many school fights among students because of what was portrayed in the movie.

Most of the teachers at the new school were nice and kind. I was very quiet and shy. I was always neatly dressed and respectful. In fact, one of my teachers, who was Caucasian, called me back into her classroom one day and said to me, "You are always so neatly dressed, have a good attitude, and if you keep that attitude, you will go a long way in life." I began to blossom into myself confidently. I believed I would become somebody special one day. The seeds of becoming brilliant were being planted in my life.

My grades began to suffer in 8th grade as I began working at a restaurant after school as a short-order cook. My mom said my older sister and I had to work to help buy school clothes and pay house bills. I was thirteen at the time.

I would be sleepy at school the next morning after working the night before. I was unable to complete my homework assignments the night before class. My eighth-grade Math teacher noticed I was sleeping in her class one day. She came over to pat me on my back, asking if I had worked the night before. I said, "yes, ma'am." She was very nice. She told me she would make sure I learned what I needed to pass her class. I barely passed my class that year. I received what was called a "social promotion."

I used to think desegregation was a good thing because it afforded me an opportunity to learn more academically. As I matured, I questioned if it was a good thing. I received a good education.

However, I am not sure it was good for our race. So many African American students began to drop out of school in the new school system. It appeared they were the ones treated most harshly by school staff.

As I matriculated through high school, I was very aware of the preferential treatment some students received compared to others. It seemed older white male teachers were allowed to use derogatory terms describing African Americans with nothing done about it.

According to school board rules, Blacks and Whites attended school together but were not allowed to attend the same prom. There was a school counselor who encouraged Black seniors to attend Technical School instead of preparing to attend college.

I learned how to cope, adapt, and finish school without getting into trouble. By the time I was a senior in high school, I started making the honor roll and graduated with a good grade point average, while I continued working almost every night during my high school years.

The first time I made the honor roll, I attended a party for students who made the honor roll. One of my Caucasian classmates thought I was not supposed to attend. As I was entering the door, she stated, "This is for students who made the honor roll." I boldly stated, "I am one of those students." She seemed surprised. She acted like I was not supposed to be at the celebration. They were accustomed to one or two African American students making honor roll each semester. She seemed shocked to see my face in the place. Afterward, I was viewed differently as someone who was smart.

There were many ways I observed the brainwashing within a system treating African Americans as if we were second-class citizens. It made me push harder to prove I was as smart as other students in my class. It wasn't until my senior year in high school I decided to apply for college at Tuskegee Institute. I heard one of my classmates say he and another classmate were going to Tuskegee Institute. He said, "You are smart; you should go to college." I did. I am so grateful my educational journey brainwashed me into brilliancy.

I still believe today; education is the key to a successful future. It doesn't guarantee success, but it affords one to compete with others who are educated in applying for a good job. I am excited about the increased rate of African Americans furthering their education receiving doctoral degrees.

The educational system can be a source of planting the seeds of brilliancy to reap a harvest of greatness in students' lives.

3. **Change the Words and Images seen by Black Males and Others:**

Words are powerful. I remember an old saying I heard back in the day. "Sticks and stones may break my bones, but words never hurt." Words do hurt. I have worked with many adult clients and patients with low self-esteem because they still hear those negative words spoken to them or about them as a child. They believed those hurtful words. Words can cut through your soul like a double-edged sword.

Children live what they learn. They learn what they live. If a child is constantly told by a parent, caretaker or any other significant person words like, "You are nothing. You will not amount up to anything. You will be a failure like your mom. Your dad is nothing, and you are just like him." These words become a self-fulfilling prophecy for children. They hear this negative reinforcement often enough; they will believe it to be true. They will act out what they hear and believe about themselves.

A self-fulfilling prophecy is a process where an originally false expectation leads to its own confirmation. In a self-fulfilling prophecy, an individual's expectation about another person eventually results in the other person acting in ways that confirm the expectation. Many times, the result is a negative outcome.

I had a client once who stated when she was a child, her grandmother would tell her she would end up like the client's own mother. The mother was described as "A no-good drug addict and alcoholic." She used drugs and her resources to purchase drugs. She prostituted her young daughter for drugs.

The daughter became a teenager hearing her grandmother tell her negative things. The teenager started presenting negative and inappropriate sexual behaviors. That teenager became an adult in treatment, disclosing how the negative talk from her grandmother reinforced her negative behaviors. She said, "I used to hear it all the time, so I started acting out what I heard."

Black males have heard negative comments from the media portraying them as criminals, lazy, gangsters and drug dealers for many years. In our society today, we are overburdened by Black-on-Black crimes, with many of the current generation of young Black males living in the poorest neighborhoods. Many of these males are uneducated and unemployed. Many of the crimes are related to drug deals gone bad. Many of these males have poor or ineffective coping skills. They are unable to manage anger, stress and resolve conflict appropriately.

I contribute this explosion of criminal behaviors to the introduction and use of violent video games, watching gangster rap music, and gangster movies as seen on BET (Black Entertainment Television), and the way social media portray Black males. The treatment of Black males by law officials has contributed significantly to negative images of black males.

Mary Ann Wilson

The video of the police murder of George Floyd was the exclamation point on how Black males are treated and viewed in American society years after slavery was abolished.

These images affect how some Black males view themselves. They also affect how others in society view Black males, therefore, resulting in indignant treatment.

The same situations and/or incidents will continue unless systemic changes are made. There must be changes made in the images presented and shown about black males.

I agree changes are being made because of having cell phones readily available to video what happens when people are treated unfairly. However, I prefer not seeing it on the national news every day. I realize news channels get higher ratings when they sensationalize the killing of people, especially African Americans. Do they have to show it over and over?

The major question is how to stop Black-on-Black crimes. Let's brainwash them to brilliancy. A brilliant person who is educated, feels good about himself, will not commit crimes usually. They will feel brilliant and do brilliant things. Some may say they will conjure up a brilliant crime and carry it out in a brilliant way. I am suggesting using brilliancy in a positive instead of negative way.

We have many brilliant people who have created and done brilliant things. Check out our African American history. You will find many past and present brilliant African Americans identified.

Let us begin to speak brilliant words in the lives of our children. Tell them every day they are brilliant. Change the trajectory of violence in our communities. Brainwash them to brilliancy.

4. **Speak Positive words to young children, especially Black males:**

As a man thinketh in his heart, so is he. Proverbs 23:7

Dr. King spoke so eloquently in his Mountain Top speech, "I dream a world where little Black boys and little Black girls are judged by the content of their character and not the color of his skin." It would be so amazing for little Black boys to awaken every morning and hear the words, "You are brilliant." Even more powerful would be to have him recite "I am brilliant" every morning when he rises out of bed and when he lays down to sleep at night. Imagine how powerful this would be.

I see the new generation of Black boys saying this every day repeatedly. I hear parents telling their sons and daughters, "you are brilliant."

The Bible says to train a child in the way he should go, and when he gets old, he will not depart from it. Parents let us start a new thing. Let's build up our children and not tear them down. Let us tell our children every day they come from a brilliant heritage. Tell them our legacy of resiliency. Tell them they can become President of this country. Tell them they are brilliant doctors, lawyers, scientists, inventors, nurse practitioners, social workers, teachers, writers, authors, entrepreneurs, or anything they want to become. Speak it into existence while they are in the womb. Studies have shown the fetus can hear while in the womb.

We must brainwash our children into brilliancy now. We cannot afford to have another generation of Black males killing themselves or each other. Statistics indicate suicide in the Black community is rising at an alarming rate. Black males ages 5 to 12 are more likely to die by suicide than any other age group.

Anyone with a positive self-image will less likely hurt themselves or anyone else. A person who believes he is brilliant will live out his own expectation of brilliancy.

Speak only positive words and brainwash our children into brilliancy.

5. Share stories of successful African American males daily to young African American boys:

When we know our history, we can have a successful present and future. We must see ourselves becoming what other brilliant people have accomplished.

A picture is worth a thousand words. When I see a beautiful African American woman on the cover of a magazine, on a television show, a commercial, on social media, in a book or a newspaper ad, I can relate and feel proud. Regardless of whether people believe they are role models, they become role models to others, especially younger generations to come.

When positive images of Black males are seen in the media instead of negative ones, we will see a decline in Black-on-Black crimes as time progresses. The new generations will not see themselves as less than others. They will feel more positive about themselves. They will strive for brilliancy. I would love to see the news broadcast more positive images of Black males instead of showing them in handcuffs being assaulted by police officers. If effective positive changes are to come, some things must change.

Earlier, I talked about going to an all-Black elementary school where all children were nurtured with high expectations to graduate becoming successful in life. There were many Black boys attending elementary school. They seemed eager to learn and succeed. It changed when we started middle and high school. It seemed more of them dropped out of school. The system was designed for them to fail. They were given the option to drop out of school at age 16. It is literally impossible to find a good-paying job at age 16 and uneducated. Many of them took that option. Many failed at life, becoming drug users and dealers. They were brainwashed into ignorance and not brilliancy.

Brilliant people will finish the course because of their expectations to accomplish great things. They will find other options instead of dropping out of school. They will be motivated to complete high school and attend college or a university of higher learning.

I realize a teenager is not an adult. The parent has a responsibility to influence a child to brilliancy. Our home environment has a major impact on our success as well. If a parent agrees to allow a child to quit high school at 16, he or she contributes to his failure to succeed and become brilliant.

There are some exceptions to every rule. My parents were not educated. I was influenced by my classmates and a neighbor in my community who attended Talladega College to get a degree in Social Work. I saw a positive role model in my community.

Young Black males must see positive role models every day to facilitate their brilliancy. Many have fathers, uncles and other male role models setting the bar high for them to follow. They must see it for it to become a part of their own worldview. It is great to see history in pages of a book. It is more impactful to witness it in everyday life.

The saying goes, "Charity starts at home and spread abroad." Children, especially Black males, must have the influence of positive role models who shows and tells them what they can become. They must see what they believe they can become in action. Being brainwashed takes time and effort. Sometimes it is obvious, and other times, it is subtle.

I have decided to use the word brilliant each time I see or talk to my grandchildren and other young children who cross my path. I find a way to say it by calling them brilliant or describing something they have done as being brilliant.

This summer, I facilitated several group sessions with a group of African American boys ages 6 to 12 where the word brilliant was used numerous times during each session to describe their behavior and had them recite the phrase, "I am brilliant." They also wrote a sentence each day where they spelled out the word brilliant using positive words.

We began and ended each session by saying, "I am brilliant." The seed of them being brilliant has been planted in their minds. I believe it will reach a great harvest in their lives. They were also shown pictures of brilliant Black males and females each session. They saw themselves and the possibilities of what they could become. They began to dream and identify how they would become brilliant as an adult.

Exposure is everything in developing a young mind to brilliancy. Exposure is one of the best forms of brainwashing children to brilliancy.

6. Use Cognitive Restructuring.

Cognitive restructuring is a technique used to help people change the way they think. It can be a tool used to help African American males think more positive thoughts about themselves. When seeing negative things portrayed in the media about African American males, they can view it only as something portrayed on social media instead of being the reality for every African American male. Their minds can be reprogramed to think and see positive images.

During the summer group sessions, the young boys heard only positive words and saw positive images about African American males who have done brilliant things.

To reconstruct the mind of young African American males, they must-see positive images of themselves reinforced in the home, school, and social media formats. They must also hear positive words being spoken to them and about them by parents, siblings, teachers, and other people with whom they associate. Children can be taught and learn they are brilliant with positive reinforcements.

7. Teach effective coping skills to brainwash to brilliancy.

I worked at a prison for eight years, teaching psychoeducational modules on effective coping skills to inmates. I learned a plethora of information on human behavior as I observed the inmate population while working at the prison. I realized many of the inmates were not taught pro-social or effective coping skills while growing up. Many of them had very low self-esteem.

Their ineffective coping mechanisms lead to poor decision-making. Many were abused as children and experienced poor parenting from their families of origin. They repeated what they had been taught. Many of them committed violent acts against others. I also realized many of them were not born with a criminal or diabolical mind. Some were not taught socially appropriate behaviors and lacked self-discipline. All of them knew the difference between right and wrong but made a choice to commit a crime.

I strongly believe if a child is taught effective ways to cope with stress, anger and resolve conflict, they will make better choices in life. It will lead to a life of brilliancy instead of violence.

Children need positive guidance, discipline, and consistency from parents. They need to hear they are loved, valued, important and held accountable for positive as well as negative behaviors. They need to be taught in early childhood there are consequences to every action.

Using effective coping skills coupled with building a positive self-image can facilitate making brilliant choices.

Mary Ann Wilson

Chapter 2
A Positive Way of Life and Roadmap to Brilliancy

Coping Skills

Coping skills are ways people adapt to life stressors, resolve conflict, and manage anger.

People use effective or ineffective ways to cope with problems. Often, many use dysfunctional coping mechanisms learned from their home environment. Children imitate what they observe in the home environment or what they see on television or social media. A child exposed to violent behavior in the home or community where they live will be more susceptible to committing violent acts.

When a child is taught positive and effective coping skills, he will most likely step into his brilliancy.

However, children consistently exposed to criminal behaviors will step into violence and commit criminal behaviors. The Black males committing crimes in our society today have witnessed many acts of violence. They have accepted a life of crime as their normalcy.

It appears as if some have little value for human life. They appear to be detached from emotions. They have rationalized in their minds that it's okay to kill another person. They have little respect for themselves, others, rules, and authority. They have little respect for elders in society. I would even say they lack spiritual guidance and support. Many do not have spiritual or religious connections. They do not attend church to learn how to love their neighbors as they are supposed to love themselves. Many appear to lack self-love with poor self-esteem.

While working as a therapist in a psychiatric hospital setting, I witnessed many young men who were drug abusers with thoughts of suicide. They seemingly cared very little about life or the value of living life to the fullest. Many presented with very poor coping skills. Many were unable to resolve conflict in prosocial ways.

To become brilliant and maintain a positive way of life, children need to learn effective coping skills.

Some of these coping skills are listed as follows:

Conflict Resolution

Conflict is a normal part of our everyday life when interacting with others. It could be as simple as disagreeing with a sibling or as complicated as having strong differences of opinion. Conflict resolution is how two or more people decide to resolve a disagreement. A positive way to resolve conflict begins by calmly communicating the disagreement with the other person involved. A negative way to resolve conflict can result in violence and the use of a weapon.

Let us begin to look at ways to resolve conflict.

1. **Acknowledge there is a conflict and/or disagreement calmly:**

Case Scenario

Bullying is a big deal with school-aged children. A 10-year-old African American male is being bullied and called negative names by a boy in his class. There are many ways he can respond. Here is one positive way to resolve this conflict.

The 10-year-old can respond using assertion skills by saying, "I feel uncomfortable when you say negative things about me. I am none of those things you called me. Let me tell you what I am. I am brilliant. I can teach you how to become brilliant too. Would you like me to show you how to become brilliant?"

Children who know they are brilliant will not take on a fight. They will be more proactive instead of reactive. They understand they are leaders and are expected to accomplish greater things in life instead of fighting with the class bully.

2. Communicate your concerns calmly and assertively:

Case Scenario

The class bully begins to yell, "You are not brilliant, and no, I don't want you to teach me how to become brilliant."

The 10-year-old calmly says, "That's fine. If you don't want to learn how to become brilliant. I will not force you. It's your choice. If you change your mind, the offer still stands."

Children should always tell an adult when they are bullied at school or on social media.

3. Express concerns in a non-accusatory way:

Case Scenario

The 10-year-old will begin to walk away, saying, "I forgive you for calling me negative names. I would appreciate it if you called me brilliant next time."

4. Discuss ways to resolve the conflict:

Case Scenario

The 10-year-old tells the class bully as he is walking away, "By the way, we will be having group sessions on being brilliant. I can tell you when our next session starts. Hope you consider attending. The group can teach you positive ways to deal with stress and other things."

5. Work on reaching a compromise:

Case Scenario

The 10-year-old says to the bully, "I can show you how to change from being angry to becoming brilliant. Reframe the word bully and replace it with brilliant.

6. Be flexible and willing to give in or walk away to facilitate a winning situation:

Case Scenario

The 10-year-old says to the bully, "Let us talk about how easy it is to change from thinking negative thoughts and replace them with positive thoughts. Man, if you change your thoughts, you can change your world. What do you think? Both of us can be brilliant. We are winners."

7. Apologize (It's okay to apologize to keep the peace):

Case Scenario

The 10-year-old says to the bully, "I hope you know I would like to be your friend. I really would like for you to join our group. I apologize if I have been talking too much about being brilliant. I care about you. I want you to know you are brilliant too. We all are brilliant in our own way."

8. Walk away from a tense situation and return when both have calmed down:

Case Scenario

The 10-year-old says to the bully, "I see you are still not sure about the things I am saying about being brilliant. All I ask is for you to think about what I am saying. If you want to talk about it later, I will be in the group session room in the building next door. We can talk later if you want to."

9. Handle situations peacefully if possible:

Case Scenario

The 10-year-old has remained calm and peaceful. He calmly walks away from the bully. He has given the bully the option to think about joining the being brilliant group sessions. He never raised his voice. He explained how the bully could find out how to tap into his brilliancy by changing negative into positive thinking.

10. Avoid violence and aggressive behaviors:

Case Scenario

Whenever someone becomes aggressive, it is better to remain calm and walk away from the situation if possible. It is never a good idea to become aggressive or use violence when someone else is doing it. Remaining calm can sometimes de-escalate situations.

People usually will not argue alone unless they have a mental illness or psychological problem. There are visible signs when a person is becoming angry. They will present with an agitated verbal tone or a threatening physical stance.

Be aware of your surroundings and walk away from hostile and violent situations. Sometimes there are ways to avoid violent situations. If you hear people arguing or someone going off on a rampage, take a different route to avoid a confrontation if possible.

Chapter 3
Anger management

The world is still in chaos with the COVID 19 Pandemic raging war on us, vicious fires burning down neighborhoods in California, increased violence, daily killings in African American communities, and we are amid the hurricane season where New Orleans had another Category 4 hurricane creating flooding among other tragedies from the storm. People are living on the edge and many experience unmanageable anger.

Many do not know how to manage anger appropriately. Some resort to violence, projecting their anger onto anyone crossing their path. Some seek out ways to express anger inappropriately. The increase in gun violence within our communities is a great indicator of poor anger management skills. Let us look at more appropriate ways to manage anger.

1. **Use appropriate communication skills:**

It's important to use effective communication skills prior to getting angry. It can prevent an anger outburst or episode. Prior to becoming angry, our nonverbal and/or body reactions began to change.

Case scenario:

You are standing in the long checkout line in Walmart when the person standing behind you starts walking closer to you, violating the safety standards of being six feet distance away from you as stated in the CDC guidelines during this pandemic.

The inappropriate way to handle the situation would be to speak to the person in an aggressive or threatening tone.

An appropriate way to communicate to the person standing behind you would be to use assertive skills by saying, "I am feeling very uncomfortable by you standing so close to me. Please step back. We are still in the middle of the coronavirus pandemic. I want to keep you and myself safe by following the CDC safety guidelines of staying six feet apart from each other."

If the person behind you is cooperative and starts stepping back in an agreeable fashion, you have communicated your needs without having a serious confrontation. However, if the person becomes irate, loud, or threatening, there are other things to consider before becoming angry.

1. **Think before you speak and act out:**

Case Scenario:

You are standing in the long checkout line at Walmart and the person standing behind you has violated the six feet safety distance space and is becoming confrontational because you asked him in a calm and non-confrontational way to step back.

You feel your heart rate begin to increase and you begin to feel yourself starting to sweat. This one is a serious dilemma. Now, you need to seriously think before you act because your body response is becoming tense and feeling threatened. It's very important at this point to decide your next response. You can start saying calming words to yourself to help you calm down and become more relaxed, or you can allow your own anger to continue to escalate. You have a decision to make. It must be a well-thought-out decision or you will find yourself amid a very serious confrontation with the person standing behind you. It's important to use positive self-talk because you feel like your safety is at risk.

You really don't know if the person behind you is carrying a weapon. You don't know his mind frame other than he is using confrontational communication after you asked him calmly to step back.

Think of ways you can de-escalate.

Always say a prayer. "God help me to calm down. I don't want to fight in this store. God help the man behind me calm down and step back as I asked him to do."

You can also start doing deep breathing exercises to help yourself calm down. Take a long, deep breath, breathing inside, holding it for three seconds and then take a long breath breathing out for three to six seconds, exhaling very slowly. Practice these deep breathing exercises two or three times until your body becomes less tense and calm. Try it. It works.

2. **Think of the consequences of your behavior:**

Case Scenario:

You have been standing in the long checkout line at Walmart with the person behind you becoming confrontational because you asked him to step back from violating your safety space of six feet distance during this COVID 19 pandemic. You have been using positive self-talk and deep breathing exercises to calm down. Hopefully, your thinking is still rational, and your body is less tense.

Now, it's important for you to think of the consequences of your behavior/response. Some of the questions going through your mind are, "Should I be confrontational with him and embarrass myself? Am I going to stand here and let this person violate my space? Is it worth it to get into a fight with him? Should I just leave the store and come back later? Do I want to cause a bigger scene? Do I want to go to jail?"

"I know if I turn around and look at him, it's going to be on. Can I be the bigger person by standing in the line and not saying anything else to him? Can I stand in front of my shopping cart instead of behind it to give myself more space by putting the shopping cart between the two of us to give more space?" This last thought is a brilliant idea.

"I don't have to talk to him. I can complete my shopping order and get out of this store." This is a winning situation.

"I can go home safely without having to get into a serious confrontation with someone who appears to be ignorant in following the safety guidelines during this pandemic. Thank you, God, for allowing me to calm down." These last thoughts will allow you to place yourself and the person behind you to be in a winning situation.

3. Do not use threatening or aggressive behavior:

Case Scenario

You have been standing in the long checkout line with a person behind you violating your personal space. Instead of standing six feet distance away, he is coming closer to you. After calmly asking him to step back, he becomes confrontational and irate.

Instead of being calm, you become threatening and irate with him. He begins using profanity and saying what all he is going to do to you. You take him on and say, "I double dog dare you to put your hands on me. I got something for you." He comes closer, and a fight begins between the two of you, resulting in the store security guard and the local police being called to separate the fight. Both of you are handcuffed in front of all the people in the store and taken to jail. As played in monopoly, you pass and go straight to jail.

Using threatening and aggressive behavior is not a brilliant idea. There are some exceptions when one must protect himself or his family. However, if there are ways to de-escalate a situation, use them. Avoid the use of threatening and aggressive behaviors when possible. Once threatening and aggressive behaviors are used, there are more consequences to follow.

4. Take a time out or walk away from confrontations:

Case Scenario:

You have been standing in the checkout line with the person behind you violating your personal space and the CDC guidelines of staying six feet distance away from people not related to you. You have calmly asked him to step back, and he became confrontational and irate.

You have an option to respond to him in a confrontational or calm manner or choose to walk away from the situation. You have options. Always remember in all situations, you have options. Options mean there is more than one choice you can make.

In this situation, you can walk away and go to the store's security officer to inform him of your concerns about the person violating your personal space and his confrontational behavior.

You also have the option to walk out of the store and leave the shopping cart in the line or push it to the service desk area. A brilliant person will figure out ways to prevent a confrontation if it is possible to do so.

Sometimes we must think outside the box during these unprecedented times. Safety is our main concern during this pandemic. If something or someone poses a threat to our safety, we want to avoid those situations at all costs.

It is better to be safe than sorry. The guy standing behind in the line is posing a safety threat. I would avoid him at all costs, even if it means leaving the line and coming back at another time. We can always come back for groceries.

However, if the person in line behind you is aggressive and carrying a weapon, he may become so agitated to pull out his weapon to shoot you and other people in the store. Nothing is unimaginable in these chaotic times. Many people are living on the edge. Always choose life over having a confrontation with a person in a Walmart checkout line who may be carrying a weapon, is ready to use it to shoot and kill you.

5. Know your limitation and anger triggers:

It's important to know your own anger triggers and limitations.

Case Scenario

You have been standing in the Walmart checkout line and this person standing behind is moving closer to you, violating your personal space. He became confrontational and threatening when you calmly asked him to step back six feet in distance away from you, as stated in the CDC guidelines for safety and protection during this COVID19 pandemic.

Now, you are saying to yourself, "I know I get irritable when I come into this Walmart store when these lines are so long." Being in the long lines at Walmart is a trigger for you. Since it is a trigger, meaning it is a sensitive area in your emotions that gets stirred up by a certain situation. When something triggers you to respond a certain way, it may lead to angry outbursts or episodes. By coming into the store during times when the lines are long, you have put yourself in a high-risk situation to be confronted by other irritable people who are easily triggered into anger outbursts.

"An ounce of prevention is better than a pound of cure."

Many people are using online shopping and having their grocery orders delivered to their homes or to their cars as they wait outside for Walmart delivery people to bring their groceries to the car. Other people shop around to find a Walmart store less busy or have smaller lines with the use of self-checkout lines.

Always remember there is more than one option to any given situation. We must be diligent in protecting our safety and our health during this pandemic. If something is a trigger for you, avoid it.

When feeling your body becoming tense, calm yourself down by using relaxation techniques:

The scenario listed above presented a tense situation when confronted by a hostile and irate person. When we feel our safety and health are at risk, we become tense and angry most of the time. It is a normal reaction given the fact we are amid the COVID 19 pandemic while the virus is mutating with highly contagious variants. It is normal to feel tense, afraid, and anxious when being outside of our home.

Situations become more tense when someone threatens our safety by getting too close and violating our space. We are more reactive when we feel threatened.

However, we can practice relaxation techniques to calm ourselves down. Deep breathing is a good exercise to practice when feeling tense. It can calm you down and help you relax very quickly.

Another way to calm yourself down is to practice positive self-talk. Using visualization of being in your happy place is another way to relax and calm down when tense. Practice these skills. Remember the saying, "Practice makes perfect." Practice may make it perfect, but practice also keeps you prepared.

It's always good to be prepared and practice ways you will handle certain situations before they occur.

Think ahead, plan and you will more than likely stay ahead in the game of life.

6. Talk to someone to express feelings of anger to de-escalate and gain clarity:

When feeling tense and angry, it's always a good idea to talk to someone who is calm and will listen to our side of the story. When we keep our feelings bottled up inside, they will eventually explode. Once we get our thoughts and feelings out in the open by talking to someone, they no longer have power over us. We can gain clarity, view situation from a different perspective, and begin to de-escalate.

Case Scenario

You have left the Walmart checkout line where someone was standing too close behind you became confrontational and threatening when you asked him to step back six feet distance away from you to not violate your personal and safety space. As you are leaving the store, you realize you are feeling very angry because your heart rate has increased, and sweat is popping out of your forehead.

You walk to your car feeling angry because you really wanted to hit the person behind you in his face. You were unable to get the groceries you needed to take home. You are asking yourself, "Should I go back into the store? Should I wait for the person to come out of the store and confront him, or should I get into my car and just go home?"

Many questions are roaming through your mind. You decide to get into your car and call your best friend on the car phone.

As you are explaining what happened in the Walmart checkout line, you are still feeling angry. Your best friend is a good listener. She listens as you explain your situation. She hears your frustration as you are talking. After talking nonstop for ten minutes. She calmly says, "Take a few deep breaths to help calm yourself down."

As you are taking slow deep breaths inhaling and exhaling, you realize your heart rate is calmer, the sweat has left your forehead and your anger is de-escalating.

Your friend is saying, "You made the right choice to leave out of the store." She says, "You can go to another store tomorrow to get groceries. I understand your angry feelings. I would have responded the same way. I am glad you are feeling calmer. I think it's best for you to leave the Walmart parking lot and return home safely. The most brilliant decision you made was to walk out of the store. You are a hero in my book. A brilliant one too."

7. Use a sense of humor to lighten the mood:

"Laughter is good medicine for the Soul."

Case Scenario

While driving home, you feel your anger dissipate. You are still talking to your friend on your car phone. Your mood is lighter. Your friend starts joking with you about how you responded to the person standing too close behind you in the store. She says, "I bet you looked at that person behind you like he was crazy, didn't you?" She laughingly says, "I bet you were nervous too, weren't you?" As your friend begins to laugh, make the mood lighter, you are calmer. You say to your friend, "Girl, I know you aren't going to ever let me live this night down, are you?" She laughingly says, "I can only imagine what your face looked like in that store. I am so glad you called me, and we talked. You are brilliant, my friend. It takes a strong person to walk away from a situation like that one. So glad you made a brilliant choice."

When feeling tense or angry, look for ways to laugh about it. Use humor to lighten the mood and de-escalate from feeling angry.

8. Identify solutions to prevent confrontations and anger outbursts:

So many people complain about problems and few people look for solutions. Brilliant people focus on the solution rather than the problem. Christians are taught to focus on how big their God is, the problem solver, instead of focusing on how big their problems are.

Case Scenario

COVID 19 impacted our lives in so many ways. It changed the

way we worshipped, how school was being taught, the way people worked, how we shopped, how we communicated with family members and how we traveled. It is still a major health and safety crisis as I am writing this book now. Many people were, and some remain angry and upset because of our lifestyle changes. Some people acted out violently, causing rises in crime rates and physical attacks on others.

Let me share my COVID 19 experience: nine of my family members and I were infected with the virus this time last year. It's been one year since we were infected and healed. None of us were angry. We are grateful to be alive. Personally, I grew closer to God, my deliverer, healer, and problem solver. As a result of my experience, I wrote a book and shared solutions, coping skills to deal with the virus while sick, and ways to manage our sanity during the pandemic.

We must be proactive/prepared before we are confronted with certain situations when we can. Certainly, there was no way we could have been personally prepared for this pandemic. However, we can learn ways to manage our anger and confrontations more effectively, especially when we know we have anger management issues. As stated earlier, an ounce of prevention is better than a pound of cure.

In the case scenario above, going to Walmart when the checkout lines are long, and the store is crowded was a trigger for the person above. He could have avoided the confrontation when he entered the store by deciding to leave returning at a different time when the store was less crowded. He also had other choices to order his groceries before going inside the store. Sometimes we must make decisions that are not comfortable or convenient to avoid a crisis or volatile situation.

9. Seek help to manage anger more effectively:

Finally, once you realize you have anger management issues, seek professional help. Unmanaged anger will lead to bigger problems if not controlled. A brilliant person will realize when there is a problem, the best thing to do is focus on the solution. There are many ways to manage anger. If all your efforts find you unable to manage your anger effectively, seek professional counseling. It's a healthy choice to make.

We live in a world of chaos, violence, and unpredictability. Our world needs less anger, hate with more love and understanding. Be a part of the solution and not the problem. Step into your greatness and brilliancy by getting help to manage uncontrollable anger. Be a light of change. Make a positive difference in your and others' lives. Learn effective ways to control anger and not allow anger to control you.

Chapter 4
Positive Self Esteem and Visual Images

Our self-esteem is based on how we view ourselves, what we think about ourselves, and the visual images we see every day.

Many people have experienced childhood trauma and abuse leading to unresolved conflict and poor self-esteem. Someone from our past has done or said something to create feelings of low self-worth. Maybe we were victims of emotional, physical, sexual abuse or neglect by our parents or caretakers. Often these events or schemas from our past affect the way we view ourselves during adulthood. Statistics indicate children who were victims of abuse or neglect are at higher risk of becoming perpetrators of the same.[1] It also states self-esteem of abused children is impacted in negative ways.[1]

A child who is a victim of abuse or neglect may have a poor self-image or very low self-worth. Our self-image is developed during our early developmental years when we are raised by our family. If a child is raised in a safe and stable home, he will develop positive self-worth. However, children brought up in abusive and unstable home environments grow up feeling unloved, unwanted, and sometimes worthless.

Many of my patients who have been victims of abuse have verbalized, "feeling like a piece of trash."

It is very difficult to live a positive lifestyle or grow into your brilliancy when experiencing feelings of low self-worth. Any behavioral therapist will help a patient understand the power of the thought process. The Bible says, "As a man thinketh, so is he." We bring into our lives what we think. Our thoughts become our feelings. Our feelings become our behavior or actions. We are always thinking, feeling, and behaving.

We do a lot of self-talk. We have daily conversations with ourselves. We are constantly telling ourselves different things about ourselves, the people around us and the world around us. When our conversations in our thought process are negative, we feel negative about who we are. However, we feel positive about ourselves when we continually think positive things about ourselves, have a positive self-image/ self-worth, and have positive conversations in our minds about ourselves. The conversations we have within ourselves can lead us into our destiny of brilliancy.

In the story of "The Little Engine That Could," the train had to constantly say to itself, "I think I can," when the engine broke down as the train was going up the hill. After repeatedly speaking those words, the train was able to go over the mountain. When we believe we can accomplish brilliant things, it begins in our thinking. Most of the time, we have heard or seen these words, "I am brilliant. I can do brilliant things. I will be brilliant." The seed must be planted before the harvest can be reaped. These thoughts lead us to step into our brilliancy.

Case Scenario

There was a little girl who was five years old when her parents divorced. She felt sad and lonely because her stable home was disrupted. She felt out of place. She felt like her world was being torn upside down. Her world was being torn apart. After her parents' divorce, she lived with her grandparents, where she experienced physical and sexual abuse by a male relative. She felt unsafe and unprotected. The little girl made a commitment to herself at age five. She said, "When I grow up, I am going to finish college, get a good job so I can take care of my children if my husband decides to leave me. I will be a good mother and not allow anyone to abuse or mistreat my children."

The little girl did not know anything about a self-fulfilling prophecy. She had a bold, brave, and brilliant thought at an early age when her life was in turmoil. This little girl grew up with feelings of low self-worth. She dealt with trust issues because of what she was exposed to as a child. She developed a lack of trust in men.

She had placed high expectations on herself. She had put a plan in place to be a provider for her children if her husband decided to leave her and her children. She somehow knew at five years old she would be resilient despite the brokenness, abuse, and instability she experienced.

The mind is so powerful and believes what we tell it.

She did not focus much on her low self-worth but rather acted it out with inappropriate sexual behavior during her teenage years by participating in premarital sex. She was never married. She was an educated woman when she became a mother. She was a single parent to her children. She was able to provide a stable home environment for her children. She was able to do what her five-year-old mind had conceived all those years back. She got a college education and raised her children.

Our words are very powerful. They speak reality into our lives. We can begin today speaking words of brilliancy. Take a pause right this moment and say to yourself, "I am brilliant."

Believe it because you are brilliant. Speak positive words of power, success, control, and all things good into your life starting now. Let go of the negativity. Reframe negativity into something positive. Make your day a brilliant one beginning now.

Visual images are extremely powerful in how we view ourselves. What we see with our eyes is believable in our minds. Children often imitate what they see their parents doing, whether good or bad. Our parents are our first teachers. If they show us love, acceptance and tell us just how brilliant we are, we will believe we can conquer the world, and we will do it.

Many times, we are brainwashed by the images we see on television, social media and in advertisements like newspapers, magazines, and books.

An example we often see is beauty described by someone who is white, skinny with long flowing hair. Just maybe this is the reason so many people are trying fad diets to lose weight. Maybe this is the reason the hair weave business is booming.

It is true, beauty is in the eyes of the beholder. We all have choices to make on how we present ourselves to the world. Natural beauty is always a winner in my book. We must decipher what is real and what is fake presented by the media. Being brilliant means deciding to be true to who we are and who we are becoming in God's sight.

Just because the media portrays Black men as criminals, it is not the identity of every black male. The images shown are very dehumanizing in many cases. It is designed to dehumanize Black men and sometimes all people of color. It would be nice to see more positive images of Black males on television and social media. The media can change the visual images portrayed to improve the plight of people of color in America.

Black males and people of color don't have to buy into what the media is selling. Choose to be brilliant despite what's portrayed. Many are making a personal choice not to become what the media portrays. It's a personal choice. It all begins in the mind frame of the person watching the image.

During slavery time, many of the slaves were in bondage physically, but their minds were free. They worked toward freedom. They came up with brilliant ideas and ways to escape from slavery. They saw themselves beyond the visual images portrayed or witnessed.

Case Scenario

One of the boys in my Brainwashed to Brilliancy group is autistic. He doesn't talk much. He listened to the group discussion on being brilliant during each session. He has the most beautiful smile and shares it with the group each time. When asked what he wanted to become when he grew up, he said, "I want to be a dad." He proudly said it with conviction.

I knew from the way he said he wanted to be a dad; his own dad was a great example to him. He wanted to imitate the visual images he saw in his own dad.

It's very important for parents to take an active role in portraying positive visual images for children to follow. Especially for Black males, the father's role in portraying positive images is vital to helping his son step into his brilliancy.

Other Coping Skills

1. Healthy Thinking Pattern

Our thoughts are very powerful. Thoughts can determine our actions. Thoughts can determine our future. If you have unhealthy thoughts, you will make unhealthy decisions. Being brilliant means thinking before you act. A brilliant person will be proactive, thinking of the consequences of his action before making a choice to act.

Practice thinking positive, affirming thoughts when awakened in the morning and throughout the day. Say positive affirming statements to yourself throughout your day. In fact, write down positive affirmations on a sticky note to put in places you can read them to yourself when you arise in the mornings. In fact, the tone of a beautiful day can be set by reading or speaking positive affirmations to yourself each day. Such affirmations may be, "I am brilliant. It's going to be a day of brilliancy. I will accomplish brilliant things today."

Remember, our thoughts become feelings. Our feelings become behaviors. We have the power to decide how our day will turn out. We set the stage for our day by what we think at the beginning of each day. We also have the power to change our thought when we realize we are having negative thoughts about our day when we awaken. We can change our thoughts to something positive.

2. Healthy Eating Patterns

Our overall health is very important. We must think, eat, and feel healthy to function daily. Children especially need a well-rounded diet of healthy thoughts and healthy foods. The saying, "We are what we eat," is very profound. Brilliancy begins in our thoughts and is nourished by a healthy diet.

3. Healthy Living Patterns

Developing healthy living patterns are conducive to becoming brilliant. A healthy and stable home environment will facilitate brilliancy in children. A child who feels valued by parents, siblings, extended family, and the community he lives in will be more apt to achieve his brilliancy. The foundation of stability has been set. Children brought up with healthy living patterns can achieve greatness. When the home environment produces healthy living patterns with expectations of brilliancy, they usually get what they expect. When we live healthy lives, usually we receive healthy results.

4. Self Sufficiency

Brilliant people must learn to be self-sufficient. A brilliant person will follow his own mind. He will not be influenced by negative stimuli. He learns to trust and depend on his own strength and powers. A brilliant person makes responsible choices. He is accountable to himself and others. He will figure out ways to become self-sufficient.

5. Leadership Skills

A brilliant person is creative and often thinks outside the norm. They will produce creative and innovative ideas. They will lead the way while others will follow.

6. Money Management

Many of us were not taught the importance of money or how to manage it. We need money to live. We cannot survive without money. We must learn how to manage money, make money, save money, invest money, and create new ideas to develop wealth in our communities.

African Americans, as a race of people, are at the lower end of accumulating wealth in the USA in comparison to the Caucasian race. There are many reasons for this disparity. There are many millionaires and more African American billionaires being created in the past few years. We must understand the power of money and how to manage it wisely. Children must be taught how to manage money effectively. Learning effective money management skills will enhance children to step into their brilliancy.

7. Entrepreneurship

Owning a business or becoming an entrepreneur has proved to be the way to becoming financially independent. Many business owners are brilliant, creative, and innovative. They develop new ideas and create new ways to live and survive. We can train our children to become innovators creating their own business and entrepreneurship. Children of today have more opportunities giving them access to create their own path to living a successful life in the future.

Slaves had fewer resources and opportunities than people have today. Yet, slaves were brilliant and innovative. They were not enslaved in their thinking and creative abilities. Many of their creations were stolen by the slave master. They were not given credit for many of their innovations.

Children of today can dream big while stepping into their brilliancy.

8. Positive Identifications/Network

There is an old saying, "You are the company you keep. Birds of a feather flock together." It's true. We become the people we hang around. It's very important to hang around positive people to reach brilliancy in life. Most of the motivational speakers have said, "If you want to learn about a person, look at the five people that person hangs around the most."

Brilliant people learn very early to hang around other brilliant people. It's important to interact with people who are on the same or higher level than yourself. A person with positive identification will hang around a person who has already accomplished great things. I have heard this saying a lot in recent months, "Your network determines your net worth."

Children must understand early the power of their network. They also must learn how to develop a net worth. Brilliant people understand both.

Parents, teachers, extended family members can teach young Black boys the power of positive identification/ network.

Chapter 5
The Impact of Spirituality on our brilliancy

Spirituality is believing there is something greater than ourselves, a higher power looking out for our best interest. It is a belief that a spirit lives within us, guiding us to a higher level of consciousness in our everyday existence. Our spirituality connects us to our God, the Father, the Son, and the Holy Spirit. It's very important to have a connection with a power higher than ourselves to step into our brilliancy.

I would debate the idea of people being brainwashed to have certain spiritual beliefs. I grew up in a religious family. I was taught the importance of having a spiritual connection with God. My father was a Baptist preacher. He was a strong believer in and a teacher of the power of God. He preached sermons about the importance of accepting Jesus Christ as our Savior. He taught my siblings and me to have a close relationship with God. We believe having a close relationship with God would guide us through life, landing safely through all the trials, tribulations, and troubles we encounter throughout our lives.

Spirituality means knowing that our lives have significance in a context beyond mundane everyday existence. It means knowing that we are a significant part of a purposeful unfolding of life in our universe.[3]

Spirituality has various religious meaning to any given group of people identified by a denomination or Christian belief. Some people worship idle or different gods. I believe in the true and living God who guides and leads me throughout my daily walk and journey. Being spiritually grounded means believing and knowing that whatever situation or circumstance I face, I will be an overcomer and victorious.

Spirituality in today's world has changed in some respects appearing to be less significant to some of the newer generations. There is a saying that speaks of generations becoming wiser and weaker. My interpretation leads me to believe it means newer generations will be wiser to worldly and weaker to spiritual beliefs.

In 2 Timothy 3:1-5, it states, "This know also, that in the last days perilous times shall come. For men shall be lovers of their own selves, covetous, boasters, proud, blasphemers, disobedient to parents, unthankful, unholy, without natural affection, trucebreakers, false accusers, incontinent, fierce, despisers of those that are good, traitors, heady, high-minded, lovers of pleasures more than lovers of God: Having a form of godliness but denying the power thereof: from such turn away."

Talk about being brainwashed in a negative way; these scriptures give a powerful description of what we are facing today. However, I still believe new generations can be brainwashed into brilliancy in positive ways.

I believe if we can find our way back to the old landmark of Spiritual upbringing where the Bible is taught in homes, families attend Sunday School and Church worship services, the new generations can be brainwashed to sound spiritual doctrines.

Our world has and continues to change, especially with the beginning of the COVID 19 pandemic. Many church doors were closed to stop the spread of the virus. In doing so, many younger generations were disconnected from worshipping God, failing to maintain a spiritual focus and discipline. Many Church services were lived streamed but did not reach the masses of people who usually attended open door Church worship services.

It appears some of the new generation lacks being spiritually connected. Some have no sense of a spiritual or power higher than themselves. Some families appear to lack spiritual guidance leaving their family and children living lives of uncertainty. It is evident in the number of increased suicide rates among young people, with a significant increase among young black males.

According to a recent study, African American boys between the ages of 5 and 12 are more likely to die by suicide than any other age group. Nationwide, suicides among Black children under age 18 have been up 71 percent in the past decade.[4]

According to a news reporter, the Journal of American Academy of Child and Adolescent Psychiatry found what researchers are calling an alarming upward trend in Black Youth suicide over the past decade.[4]

A person who has no spiritual grounding or foundation has little hope in solving some of the major problems they are experiencing. They see no solutions to their current situation, lack hope and may choose suicide as the only option to solve the problem.

A person with a strong spiritual foundation will believe their faith and hope in God will give them strength to endure or deliver them from the problems they face despite seeming monumental at the time. A person of Faith believes their faith will carry them through any crisis they encounter.

Strong faith must be tested and proven. A strong Christian believer understands the scriptures in Job 14: 1-2. "Man that is born of a woman is of few days and full of trouble. He cometh forth like a flower and is cut down: he fleeth also as a shadow, and cometh not."

A non-believer, a person who does not worship God or a power higher than himself, will battle his problems alone. This can be overbearing and overwhelming, leaving a person carrying the weight of the world on his shoulder. It is too much to bear alone. We all need God to help us bear our burdens. It's alright to be brainwashed into believing in the almighty God, the author and finisher of our faith.

We must trust God to have our best interest in mind. He will not put more problems on us than we can bear. He knows everything about us because he made us. The Christian believer knows there is no testimony without a test. We will be tested daily. The more we lean on and trust God, the stronger we become in dealing with the changes confronting us daily. We can embrace all changes with God on our side. Choose to be brainwashed by God. Let him guide and lead you through this journey called life into your brilliancy.

Who Is God, and how does knowing Him impact our brilliancy?

God is our heavenly father. He is conceived as the supreme being, creator and sustainer of the universe. He is described as the Higher power. He is infinite, the beginning and the ending. He created us in His image. He created us to be brilliant. We are wonderfully made by God. In my search for who is God, I found this description below to identify who God is to us.[5]

God is...

The Creator and King.

He created all things with the awesome power and rules over His creation. Genesis 1-2, Psalm 47, Colossians 1:16.[5] This means God created everything. He is ruler over the earth and everything it inhabits. We belong to God. He is King of kings and Lord of Lord. God created our mind where he dwells within us. We are brilliantly made by God.

All-Powerful (Omnipotent)

He can Do anything. Job 42:2 Jeremiah 32:17 God has unlimited power.[5] He has the power to change our lives in a twinkling of an eye. He can do anything. He can change the trajectory for young African American males in a split second. God is almighty. Christians who trust in Him know He has the power to make our days bright and sunny even when there are rainy days. He gives us hope for better things to come.

Having a spiritual connection with God, our power source, will help lead us into a life of brilliancy.

All-Knowing (Omniscient)

He knows everything, including the thoughts and deeds of all people. Psalm 139: 1-6; 2 Corinthians 5:9-11.[5]

God knows everything about us. He knew us before we were born. He knows our past, present and our future. He already has great rewards for those who are obedient to His word. God is not asleep. He knows if there is good or evil in the hearts of men. He sees the things we do in public and private. He knows the unjust treatment some people have received. He will reward us according to our works. If we have treated others unjustly, we will receive our just reward. No one gets a free ticket to treat God's creation wrongly. Payday will come after a while.

God knows we all were designed to reach our brilliancy in life.

However, to become brilliant, we must be willing participants. We must become a part of our own rescue. We cannot wait for others to give us what is rightfully ours. We must be willing participants. We must do our part for God to step into the situation. Remember the saying, "If you take one step, God will take two." We are to be proactive, take and make steps to become brilliant. All things are possible with God. He is so powerful. He already knows the end results of His creation.

HOLY

He is absolutely sinless and does not tolerate any violation of what is right. Psalm 99:3-5, Revelations.4:8.[5]

God is Holy. He is always right and never wrong. He does not like it when we sin or mistreat each other. He hates sin because it enslaves us. Sin will eventually destroy us. A person who is holy also hates sin. It is impossible to love sin, mistreat others, witness the mistreatment of others, and claim to be holy. It's an abomination to God. A brilliant person does not want God to feel this way about him. Rather, a brilliant person wants to live a holy life, one acceptable to God.

LOVING

Christ's death and resurrection demonstrate God's great love for His people. John 3:16; 15:13; 1 John 4:8.[5]

God is love. He loves us so much He gave us His only begotten son to walk on this earth to be our earthly and spiritual connection to Him. We cannot reach a life of brilliancy with a heart filled with hate.

We must love ourselves first. Then we can show love to others. When we love ourselves, we release excessive baggage stepping into our brilliancy with less weight to carry. Sometimes it takes years before past hurts and pains are released. Americans must learn to love all people regardless of race, ethnicity, color, creed, nationality, or any other divisive label designed to separate people. Be brilliant. Choose love over hate.

A MERCIFUL AND JUST FATHER

Like any loving parent, he seeks the best for His children and will discipline them toward the end. John 14:21-23; Hebrews, 12:5-11.[5]

God is merciful. He is a just father to his children. He wants what is best for us. Like our earthly father, God will discipline those He loves. Those who mistreat others will be disciplined by God. Often to reach our brilliancy in life, we must be disciplined by God. We also must discipline ourselves to be set apart from the ordinary to become extraordinary. Brilliant people stand away from the crowd.

THE TRINITY

The Father, Son, and Holy Spirit are one, in essence, three in function: They all work together to bring about human salvation. Titus 3:4-66.[5]

As Christians, we are connected to the trinity. We cannot experience one without the other as we walk into our destiny of brilliancy. Our spirits must connect with like-minded spirits in love.

God is so many different things. He impacts every aspect of our lives. We must depend on Him to direct our path. We must ask God to order our steps. We know the steps of a good man are ordered by God. Trust God to lead you into your brilliancy.

His Presence allows you to step into your brilliancy

The most sacred and divine feeling is knowing God's presence surrounds every aspect of your being. Your mind, body and soul feel a sense of peace and unspeakable joy like you have never experienced. Living your best life to the fullest each day requires being in the presence of God. Every day I wake up, I realize God allowed me to see another day. He allowed me to be alive and experience His goodness. He allowed me to experience my health, my sight, my mobility, my positive thoughts, my positive mood, and my ability to give him gratitude for being my heavenly father. His presence allows me to worship him in spirit and truth.

Again, I must share my COVID 19 experience to express just how aware I am of the presence of God.

I was home alone physically when I realized I was infected with the virus last year. Initially, I was afraid my family and I would die because of news reports of the virus's impact on the world, especially African Americans dying at higher rates than other races.

It was only when I tapped into my Spirituality, I realized the presence of God surrounding me when I was sick. I was able to overcome my fears by tapping into my Faith. I realized I was not alone spiritually. I felt the presence of God all around me when I was sick and unable to move because the virus had taken away my strength. God carried me and the rest of my family to healing from the virus.

Now, every day I experience, I am consciously aware of God's presence in my life. I feel His spirit keeping me safe and calm amidst all the chaos in the world surrounding us. I can enjoy the moment without hesitation, fear, and anxiety. I submitted all my cares to God. His presence surrounds me daily.

To reach your brilliancy in life, allow the presence of God to surround you. Our young African American males must understand the presence of God surrounds them. They must understand the importance of having a relationship with God, a power higher than themselves. They must know they were created by God to become brilliant.

His purpose for you is to live a life of brilliancy

God created man for His glory. God created us to worship Him in spirit and truth. We were not designed to worship ourselves. We were not designed to mistreat and mislead others. We were designed to love and not hate each other. When we love each other the way God loves each of us, we are destined for greater things from God. Fulfill your God-given purpose of brilliancy. Start walking into it by planting the seed in your thought process. Remember, thoughts are powerful. Our mind believes what we say to ourselves. Tell yourself, "I am brilliant. I am becoming brilliant. Brilliancy is my destiny." Believe it and you will become it!

His Plan for Our Lives

God's plan for you is for better things to come your way. When we live a purpose-driven life with God as our pilot, we will prosper and reach higher heights than ever imagined. God's words say in Jeremiah 29:11, "For I know the plans I have for you," declares the Lord. "Plans to prosper you and not harm you. Plans to give you hope and a future."[5]

We are all destined for a life of brilliancy. It has already been spoken by God. Our job is to believe it in our minds and achieve it in our works. The steps of a good man are ordered by the Lord. I say to you reading these words, "Step into your brilliancy right now if you have not started. Wake up with the thought and plan to be brilliant today. Ask yourself these questions, "How will I activate my brilliancy plan today? How will I help others tap into their brilliancy today? What brilliant words will I use today? What brilliant steps will I take today?

A life of brilliancy requires thinking ahead, planning, and staying ahead in the game called life.

God's plan for our life was already developed before we were born. His plan is unfolding every moment we breathe. He is putting all the pieces of the puzzle together as we live our lives daily. He knows our steps to brilliancy are ordered and orchestrated by Him.

Be bold, brave, and bodacious. Ask God about His plans for your life. He will reveal it piece by piece in His own perfect timing. God will not reveal the total picture of our puzzle until we can receive it. He will not put more on us than we can bear. His plans are orchestrated to give us what we need when we need it. Trust God's plan and timing. He will never let us fall to a point where we cannot get back up if we lean and depend on Him. His grace, mercy and favor are His works of brilliancy in our lives.

Brilliant people think, plan, and stay ahead!

Chapter 6
The Role of The Black Female

The Black female has a pivotal role in influencing children to reach their brilliancy. Our mothers are our first teachers. Many do an excellent job of raising responsible, law-abiding children. Many of the Black families are headed by single mothers who work full-time jobs while raising their children. The mother's role has been focused on nurturing and providing emotional support for children. Many reports, including the Moynihan report of 1965, have suggested the Black family is matriarchal in structure, meaning even in married families, the Black female is the head.

I have always believed a man is the head of the family based on my Christian upbringing. The Bible also states in Ephesians 5:21-32, "Submitting yourselves one to another in the fear of God. Wives, submit yourselves unto your own husbands, as unto the Lord. For the husband is the head of the wife, even as Christ is the head of the church: and he is the savior of the body."

A mother's role is very significant in raising children in the family. Traditionally, the husband's role is to be a provider and protector. The mother's role is to be the nurturer, teacher and provider of all the other needs of her children.

The Black female role has changed some over the years with so many single women head of the household where the father is absent. **The Black female** has been the glue to keep the family going.

Even in married families, the mother has a significant impact in raising the children. When a son has developed a good relationship with his mother, he usually can have a good relationship with his own wife or other significant women in his life. A man who experiences a conflictual relationship with his mother will have conflictual relationships with other women in his life.

It's very important for the mother to love, nurture and discipline her children. It's important for children to hear positive words spoken to them daily by their mothers.

The Black female is essential to raising brilliant Black children. Even during slavery, Black women were nannies, nurturing and nursing the master's white children.

Black women are making many strides in education, the workforce and increasing income. Many Black females are setting an example of how successful and brilliant their children can become. There is an old saying the apple doesn't fall too far from the tree. Children learn what they live. They live what they learn. Our children need to hear the words "You are brilliant" every day from their mothers and other significant people in their lives.

Chapter 7
The Role of The Black Male

The role of the Black Father is so important for children to grow up feeling positive about themselves. A father is the leader in the family. He gives his children an identity of where they come from and what they can become. His children will emulate what they see him do in many situations. A father must have a positive influence on the children's life. We have many people who experience a sense of brokenness because of not having their fathers actively involved in their lives. They experience abandonment and trust issues.

A son who experiences his father's presence in the home will learn how to become a man. He will also learn how to treat other women based on the way he observes his father treating his mother. A daughter will also learn how a man should treat a woman by observing how her father treats her mother. She will expect to be treated like a princess/queen if she observes her father treating her mother this way.

It's extremely important for young black males to be surrounded by positive black male role models. Many young black males have become successful because of being around positive black males who may have been surrogate father figures. Some black males have taken on the role of Big Brother or mentor. These roles have been a significant catalyst to help build self-esteem in and empower young black boys.

The Black male must take an active role in building Black boys into brilliant men.

Chapter 8
The Role of the Black Family

The traditional structure of the Black family has changed significantly over the years due to the diversity in family living arrangements. The traditional family of husband, wife and children still exists but is on the decline with families in America. Many Black children live in single-parent homes, which may include a single-parent living with an unmarried partner.

Many of the single parents are working and struggling to raise their children. Many of the single-parent families are grandparents raising grandchildren. Many children are raised by extended family members as well.

The biological and extended family members are vital to raising the next generation of brilliant children. There are many problems and issues confronting the Black family. This book is more solution focused.

The Black family has survived despite all odds placed against it. Many could have given up considering the maltreatment during slavery and even now in the present day. However, with all the different family types, Black families are still strong and surviving.

Our family, community, and neighborhood have made significant impacts on the Black community. We rely on each other for survival. **The Black family** is the catalyst to help our future generations step into their brilliancy.

Chapter 9
Rebuilding the Village

An African proverb or saying indicates, "It takes a village to raise a child." It means it takes an entire community of different people interacting with children for them to grow up safely in their environment. I often wondered what happened to the village. I grew up in a community where everyone in the community looked out for the children within the community. We had our village back then.

When I was a teenager, my mother worked at night, leaving my siblings and me home until she returned from work. There were older neighbors around who would watch out for us, making sure we didn't get into trouble or leave home while my mother was working. They also made sure other children, especially boys, were not coming to our house.

One older lady named Mrs. Jo lived across the street from us. She would sit on her front porch, watch us, making sure we were inside the home when the streetlights came on at dusk. She could discipline us if we got out of line. She would tell my mother the next day if she had to correct us in any way. If she told my mother about us misbehaving, we would get a whipping with a switch. My mother didn't question us about our behavior. She would tell us to go outside to get our own switch to whip us on our legs or our backside. There was no such thing as children calling the police because a parent whipped or disciplined them, as many parents experience now with the new generations of children.

The village included the neighborhood alcoholic or drunkard, as we called him. He would be drunk on alcohol, but he, too, would watch over/ protect the children in the neighborhood. There were no strangers coming into the neighborhood and abducting children.

The village included immediate, extended family members consisting of grandparents, aunts, uncles and cousins, all neighbors in the community, the community store, church members, preachers, teachers, coaches, the local barbershop, and classmates. All adults in these groups could discipline children if they misbehaved. Children knew they would get in trouble twice if someone disciplined them and told their parents. Many children got two whippings in one day. One was from someone in the community and another from their parents for misbehaving.

I often wonder if it is possible to rebuild the village. I believe in possibilities. Our children, especially young black males, would stop the violence if structure, concern, and more value were built back into our communities. I am usually not a pessimist. However, I am not sure the young black males killing each other would be receptive to changing their worldviews about their lifestyle.

I believe we can start a change with the newest generation of young Black males ages 3 to 12. We can teach them better coping and life skills to brainwash them into brilliancy.

I believe we can build a community of people to care for and value them the way we were valued as children growing up in my community.

I believe I am a change agent. I can implement my program of brilliancy to make a positive difference in the lives of Black children, especially young Black males.

I am facilitating change by letting them know they were born to become brilliant. I am teaching them about our heritage of strength, endurance, sustainability, stamina, spiritual connectedness, self-sufficiency, having a purpose-driven life, and survival skills. I believe we can rebuild the village. We must rebuild the village to save our children and future generations to come.

CONCLUSION

Stepping into brilliancy requires planting good seeds, thoughts, and ideas into our children's minds. We must awaken daily feeling motivated to be all we are destined to be. We must brainwash ourselves into our brilliancy. Parents and caretakers, teachers, family, friends, siblings, and everyone in our circle can start speaking brilliant words first to themselves and then to the children in our lives.

We come from a heritage of resiliency and brilliancy. Somewhere down the line, some of us started believing negative things we heard about who we are as a people. Some people believe the negative images portrayed on social media about us. Some have taken on the role of the oppressor and started oppressing each other. That's the slave mentality. We are not slaves anymore.

We must flip the script, reframe the negativity, and move toward self-love, self-value, self-appreciation, and self-acceptance.

Our history is strong and powerful. Yes, we have a history of slavery, but it's not our legacy. Let's look back at our history before we became slaves. We must start looking beyond slavery if we are to recover from it. I realize systemic racism still exists. Some people want us to stay in the slave mentality. It's more than time to change for the better by stepping into a destiny of brilliancy.

Black males are brave, brilliant, powerful, and resilient. We must tap into our brilliancy and put those guns down. Be Black and proud. **Remember**, you were created in the image of God. God designed you to be resilient and brilliant.

God's plan is to prosper you and give you hope for better things to come. God's plan is for you to use your brilliant mind to love, help, serve, and respect each other. We will win with God on our side. Take a leap of Faith. Let God lead and brainwash you into brilliancy.

We can and we must recover from slavery as a nation. We are all impacted by the way we treat each other. I have shared my recovery plan. My plan is only a beginning. We can all work together to develop our own individual plan to step into our brilliancy.

Join me on this journey to make our communities safer and less violent. Together we can stop the violence. We can stop Black-on-Black crimes in future generations by teaching positive coping skills and effective ways to resolve conflict and manage stress and anger.

Together, we can change the trajectory for African American males by reaching and teaching them early about their brilliancy. We can build a positive self-image in our children by giving them a spiritual foundation, teaching them to love themselves the way God loves them because they are created in the image of God first. Then we can teach them our strong legacy of survival, strength, and endurance. We can show them their history of brilliancy. We can teach them not to believe the negative images portrayed on social media. We can prepare them for a life of brilliancy by telling them every morning, **"You are brilliant."**

Section 11

Workbook Activity

Complete the activities on the next pages to begin stepping into your brilliancy.

Brainwashed To brilliancy Activity

Take a journey into your brilliancy. Discover just how brilliant you are or becoming.

Step into your brilliancy by describing yourself using all positive words spelling out the word

B R I L L I A N T

Begin with the first letter **B** and end with **T.** How brilliant are you? Challenge yourself by coming up with as many positive words as you can with each letter in the word Brilliant to describe who you are now or who you are becoming! Celebrate You! You are destined for greatness! **You are Brilliant!!!**

Example: **B = Bold, Brave, Beautiful**

B_____

_____

_____

_____

_____

_____

_____

_____

_____

Name a famous African American whose first, middle or last name begins with the letter B. List the ways they are brilliant by their name:

Example:

    1. Barack Obama 44th President of the United States, Civil Rights Activist, Nobel Peace Prize Winner

    2.

    3.

    4.

Example: R= Resourceful, Resilient, Respectful

R _____

_____

_____

_____

_____

_____

_____

_____

_____

_____

Name a famous African American whose first, middle or last name begins with the letter R. List the ways they are brilliant by their name.

Example:

1. Rosa Parks Civil Rights Activist from Montgomery, Ala. She refused to give up her seat on the bus to a white passenger on December 1, 1955.

2.

3.

4.

Mary Ann Wilson

Example: I= Important, Innovative, Intelligent

I _____

   _____

   _____

   _____

   _____

   _____

   _____

   _____

   _____

   _____

Name a famous African American whose first, middle or last name begins with the letter I. List the ways they are brilliant by their name:

Example:

    1. Allen Iverson   Professional Basketball player

    2.

    3.

    4.

Example: L= Loving, Liberated, Likable

L _____

_____

_____

_____

_____

_____

_____

_____

_____

Name a famous African American whose first, middle or last name begins with the letter L. List the ways they are brilliant by their name:

1. Louis Farrakhan — Leader, political activist, head of Nation of Islam

2.

3.

4.

Mary Ann Wilson

Example: L=Loyal, Legendary, Listener

L _____

_____

_____

_____

_____

_____

_____

_____

_____

Name a famous African American whose first, middle or last name begins with the letter L. List the ways they are brilliant by their name:

Example:

1. LeBron James Professional Basketball player and philanthropist

2.

3.

4.

Example: I=Intuitive, Inspirational, Involved

I _____

_____

_____

_____

_____

_____

_____

_____

_____

_____

Name a famous African American whose first, middle or last name begins with the letter I. List the ways they are brilliant by their name:

Example:

1. Ida B. Wells American Journalist, educator, and civil rights activist

2.

3.

4.

Example: A=Awesome, Artistic, Able

A _____

_____

_____

_____

_____

_____

_____

_____

_____

Name a famous African American whose first, middle or last name begins with the letter A. List the ways they are brilliant by their name:

Example:

1. Muhammed Ali   Born Cassius Clay, Heavyweight Boxing Champion, Civil Right Activist

2.

3.

4.

Example: N=Nice, Nifty, Noteworthy

N _____

_____

_____

_____

_____

_____

_____

_____

_____

Name a famous African American whose first, middle or last name begins with the letter N. List the ways they are brilliant by their name:

Example:

1. Nelson Mandela South African anti-apartheid revolutionary, political leader, first President of South Africa from 1894-1999, Nobel Peace Prize Winner

2.

3.

4.

Example: T=Truthful, Trustworthy, Talented

T _____

_____

_____

_____

_____

_____

_____

_____

_____

Name a famous African American whose first, middle or last name begins with the letter T. List the ways they are brilliant by their name:

Example:

1. Booker T. Washington   Founder of Tuskegee Institute and National Negro Business League

2.

3.

4.

Note: Add to your list of brilliant words as you think of them. Even if you list only one word, you are still brilliant. Your level of brilliancy does not exist on quantity but the quality of your actions and your belief in who you are or who you are becoming.

Every morning when you awaken, stare into the mirror and speak a positive affirmation to yourself. Say to yourself, "I am brilliant. Today, I will accomplish brilliant things." As you go about your daily journey, look for something brilliant in others. Tell them the brilliant things you see in them. Make somebody's day with a random kind word. Speak brilliancy into the lives of others.

Parents, guardians, and teachers tell your children and students daily, "You are brilliant." Tell them what you observe as brilliant about them. If we want to combat black-on-black crime and decrease the suicide rate among our children, we must start telling them how valuable they are to us and to the world. We must implant positive things into their minds very

early. We are the village.

Remember, we must activate what we want our children to imitate.

We must plant a positive seed if we want to reap a positive harvest.

Be Brilliant.

You are designed by God.

You are special.   You are resilient.

You have been "Brainwashed To Brilliancy Recovering From Slavery" !!!!!!!

Daily Reflection Notes of Brilliant Thoughts, Ideas, and Actions

Take a weekly Journey into Brilliancy

Day 1 Describe your experience or expression of brilliancy today.

_____

_____

_____

_____

_____

_____

_____

_____

_____

_____

Day 2 Describe your Journey to Brilliancy today

Day 3 Describe your Journey to Brilliancy today

Day 4 Describe your Journey to Brilliancy today

Day 5 Describe your Journey to Brilliancy today

Day 6 Describe your Journey to Brilliancy today

Day 7 Describe your Journey to Brilliancy today

Upon completing your one-week journey, say hello to your brilliancy by writing a letter of reflection to yourself. Describe how you have changed during this week. Include your feelings, mood, how your thoughts have changed and what actions you have taken for yourself or assisted a child to step into his brilliancy. Write your letter below! Use the feelings chart below if needed.

REFERENCES

1. Psychodynamics | Definition of Psychodynamics by Merriam-Webster. Assessed August 9, 2021. https://www.merriam-webster.com/dictionary/psychodynamics.

2. Cognitive Restructuring l Definition of Cognitive Restructuring by Concordia University. Accessed August 10, 2021. https://www.concordia.ca

3. Spencer, M (2012) What is Spirituality/A personal exploration

   Royal College of Psychiatrists. Assessed August 10, 2021 www.rcpsych.ac.uk

4. Robinson, P. (WAFB). Suicide numbers in the Black Community rising at an alarming rate.

   10TV Web Staff. Journal of American Academy of Child Psychology and Adolescent Psychiatry reports upward trend in Black Youth Suicide over past decade. Assessed September 9, 2021. 10tv.com.

5. Who is God? l Visual.ly. Assessed September 28, 2021. https://visual.ly/community/Infographics/education/who-god

For more information or to contact the author

www.maryawilson.com

Marywilson1459@gmail.com

Ever-true1@yahoo.com

LinkedIn

Instagram

Saving Ourselves Saving Our Sons Inc.

334-593-3027

334-462-9425

www.ingramcontent.com/pod-product-compliance
Lightning Source LLC
Chambersburg PA
CBHW050843160426
43192CB00011B/2135